discovermore

Earth's Biomes

A Look at Tropical Rainforests

Dwayne Hicks

Britannica®
Educational Publishing
IN ASSOCIATION WITH
THE ROSEN PUBLISHING GROUP

Published in 2027 by Britannica Educational Publishing (a trademark of Encyclopædia Britannica, Inc.) in association with The Rosen Publishing Group, Inc.
2544 Clinton Street, Buffalo, NY 14224

Distributed exclusively by Rosen Publishing.
To see additional Britannica Educational Publishing titles, go to rosenpublishing.com.

Editor: Greg Roza
Book Design: Michael Flynn

Photo Credits: Cover Narmeria/Shutterstock.com; (series background) Dai Yim/Shutterstock.com; p. 5 (top) JLugonStudio/Shutterstock.com; p. 5 (bottom) gg-foto/Shutterstock.com; p. 6 Influez Studio/Shutterstock.com; p. 7 GUDKOV ANDREY/Shutterstock.com; p. 8 Designua/Shutterstock.com; p. 9 Bertrand Godfroid/Shutterstock.com; p. 10 Mrs Fine Stock/Shutterstock.com; p. 11 Gabriel Spenassatto/Shutterstock.com; p. 12 Ahmd k/Shutterstock.com; p. 13 guentermanaus/Shutterstock.com; p. 14 Arcady/Shutterstock.com; p. 15 Rostasedlacek/Shutterstock.com; p. 17 (top) Petr Muckstein; p. 17 (bottom) worldswildlifewonders; p. 18 juerginho/Shutterstock.com; p. 19 MLeCharpentier/Shutterstock.com; p. 20 GUDKOV ANDREY/Shutterstock.com; p. 21 https://commons.wikimedia.org/wiki/File:28_05_2021_-_Foto_do_dia_(51211347161).jpg; p. 22 Miroslav Srb/Shutterstock.com; p. 23 Narong Khueankaew/Shutterstock.com; p. 24 aoya/Shutterstock.com; p. 25 Teo Tarras/Shutterstock.com; p. 27 (top) Rich Carey/Shutterstock.com; p. 27 (bottom) germanoandrade/Shutterstock.com; p. 28 PARALAXIS/Shutterstock.com; p. 29 My Good Images/Shutterstock.com.

Cataloging-in-Publication Data

Names: Hicks, Dwayne.
Title: A look at tropical rainforests / Dwayne Hicks.
Description: New York : Britannica Educational Publishing, in association with Rosen Educational Services, 2027. | Series: Discover more: Earth's biomes | Includes glossary and index.
Identifiers: ISBN 9781641906418 (library bound) | ISBN 9781641906401 (pbk) | ISBN 9781641906425 (ebook)
Subjects: LCSH: Rain forest ecology--Juvenile literature. | Biotic communities--Juvenile literature.
Classification: LCC QH541.5.R27 H68 2027 | DDC 577.34--dc23

Manufactured in the United States of America

Some of the images in this book illustrate individuals who are models. The depictions do not imply actual situations or events.

CPSIA Compliance Information: Batch #CSBRIT27. For further information contact Rosen Publishing at 1-800-237-9932.

Contents

Forests of the World

A biome is a large region of Earth that has a certain climate and certain types of living things. Major biomes include tundra, forests, grasslands, and deserts. Tropical rainforests are also one of Earth's biomes.

There are several forest biomes. The taiga is a conifer forest biome, found in cold northern areas. Deciduous forests are found mainly in the Northern Hemisphere, south of the taiga, but north of tropical forests. Deciduous forests have four seasons and lose their leaves in the fall.

Thick forests found in wet areas of the world are called rainforests. There are several kinds of rainforests. Montane rainforests, or cloud forests, grow in mountainous regions. Temperate rainforests grow in cool parts of the world, such as the northwestern United States and southern Australia. Monsoon rainforests have a dry season and trees that shed their leaves each year. They grow in Southeast Asia.

The tropical forest biome has great wildlife diversity. This means that many kinds of plants and animals live there.

compare and contrast

What do tropical rainforests have in common with other types of forests? In what ways are they different?

Waimea Canyon on the Hawaiian island of Kaua'i features a montane rainforest. It's one of the rainiest places in the world.

The most familiar rainforests are hot, tropical forests filled with trees that stay green year-round. Tropical rainforests lie near the **equator**. This biome has hot, wet conditions all year long. Tall, tropical trees and many other plants grow there.

The Cigenter River in Java, Indonesia, flows through a densely packed, protected tropical rainforest.

Who do you think will win this battle between rainforest predators: the caiman or the anaconda?

Tropical rainforests are known for the diversity of their plants and animals. Scientists think that more than half of the world's plant and animal species, or types, live in tropical rainforests. Monkeys, parrots, jaguars, and anaconda snakes are just a few of the many rainforest animals. There may be many species that have not yet been discovered!

WORD WISE

THE EQUATOR IS AN IMAGINARY CIRCLE AROUND EARTH. IT DIVIDES EARTH INTO TWO EQUAL PARTS: THE NORTHERN HEMISPHERE AND THE SOUTHERN HEMISPHERE.

Where in the World?

Tropical rainforests are found in parts of the tropics that get more than 70 inches (180 centimeters) of rain each year. The tropics is the wet, hot biome near the equator.

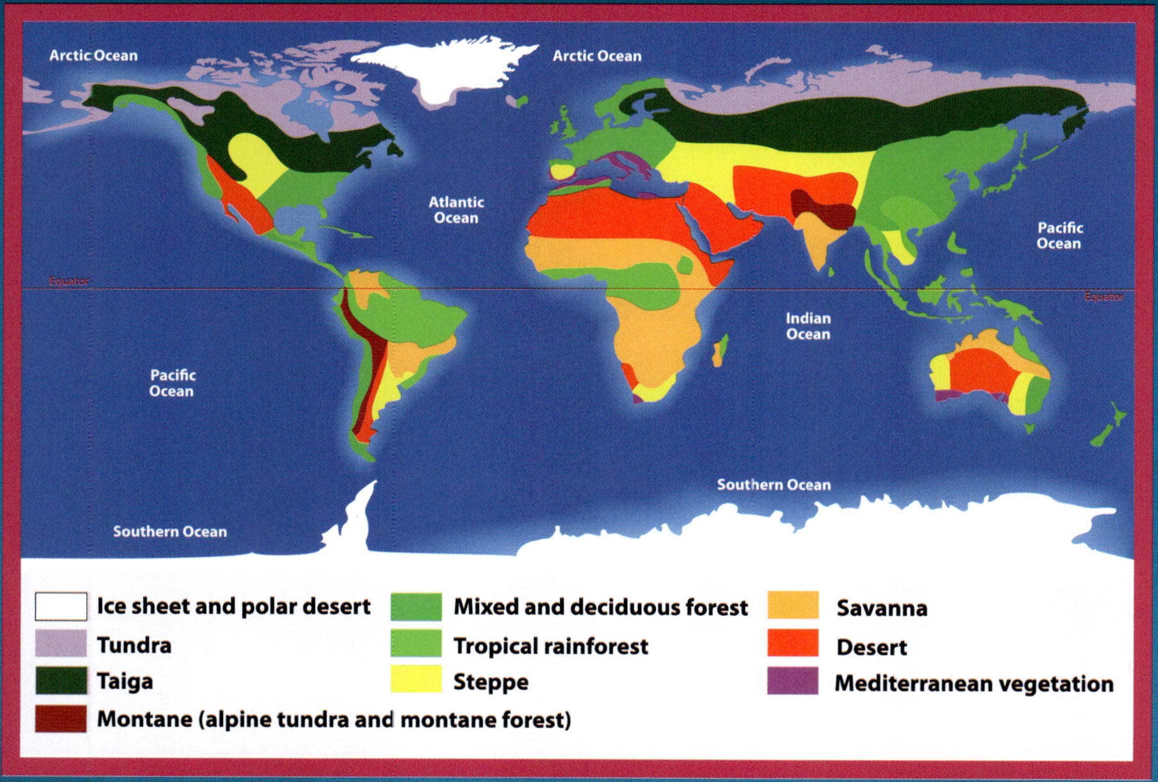

Earth's tropical rainforests are all near or on the equator.

The rainforest in the Congo is home to the endangered mountain gorilla.

Parts of South America and Central America, western and central Africa, Southeast Asia, and Australia have tropical rainforests. The world's largest rainforest is located in the Amazon River basin of Brazil. It covers about 40 percent of that country. However, tropical rainforests cover less than 5 percent of Earth's total land surface.

The second largest tract of rainforest is in central Africa, in the region around the Congo River. Almost half of the tropical rainforests in this tract are in the Democratic Republic of the Congo. The largest tropical rainforests in Asia are found in New Guinea and parts of Borneo.

Consider This

Desert and grassland biomes get less rain than tropical rainforests. Why do you think more rain leads to rainforest biomes?

Top to Bottom

Tropical rainforests are made up of distinct levels. At the top of the forest is a thick layer called the canopy. It is formed by the spreading branches and thick leaves of tall trees. The canopy blocks much of the sunlight from the area below. The canopy can be between 100 and 170 feet (30 and 50 meters) above the ground. A few very tall trees stick up above the rest of the canopy. They are called emergent trees. Many animals live among the treetops of the canopy. These include insects, birds, and mammals.

The Amazon River is visible beyond the thick, lush canopy of the Amazon Rainforest.

Plants that grow in the low light of the rainforest understory also grow well in pots in people's homes. These include philodendrons and zebra plants.

The section below the canopy is called the understory. It contains small trees and saplings, or young trees. Their stems reach up toward the light. However, these smaller trees generally do not receive enough sunlight to grow into adult trees. The understory also includes shrubs, plants, and vines.

Consider This

Why do you think many animals make their homes in the canopy?

The rainforest floor is usually dark because the canopy and understory block so much sunlight. Therefore, only plants that can tolerate shade grow there. So little sunlight reaches the ground that the forest floor may be only lightly covered by ground vegetation. There may be open spaces between the tree trunks. If one of the trees that creates the canopy dies or falls, a gap may open in the canopy, allowing sunlight to reach farther down into the forest. In such cases the ground vegetation may become thick and dense.

This plant sprouted on the dark floor of a tropical rainforest.

The constant rain washes away many of the **nutrients** in the soil. To make up for that loss, bacteria, fungi, and insects on the forest floor help to break down dead plants and animals. This process creates a thin, rich top layer of soil that provides nutrients to the roots of the plants and trees. Many rainforest trees have shallow root systems because of this.

WORD WISE

NUTRIENTS ARE SUBSTANCES THAT LIVING THINGS NEED IN ORDER TO SURVIVE AND GROW.

Rainforest Plants

Many tropical rainforest trees stay green all year, though they do shed their leaves sometimes. Palms are among the most common trees in the tropical rainforest.

Lliana pants get closer to the sunlight by climbing trees!

The rainforests in Southeast Asia are home to plants called *Nepenthes*, or tropical pitcher plants. These plants eat meat! Insects and small animals crawl or fall into the "pitcher" where they are trapped and digested by the plant.

Below the thick canopy, other plants have to compete with each other to get enough light. As a result, many plants use other plants to reach toward the sunlight. For example, woody plants called lianas attach to the stems of other plants and climb from the ground to the canopy. Epiphytes, or air plants, are also abundant in the rainforest. These plants are not attached to the ground. They live on other plants. They get water and minerals from rain and also from debris that collects on the supporting plants. Mosses, ferns, and orchids can often be found attached to larger plants.

Consider This

Why do you think that epiphytes have been so successful in tropical rainforests? What advantage might there be in not having roots attached to the ground?

Rainforest Animals

Just a tiny part of a tropical rainforest can contain thousands of animal species. Many plant-eating animals live in the canopy—for example, monkeys, flying squirrels, and sharp-clawed woodpeckers. At the lower levels of the forest are animals that run, flutter, hop, and climb in the understory. On the rainforest floor are such animals as chimpanzees, gorillas, elephants, pigs, deer, and leopards.

Many animals in the rainforest have unusual characteristics. For example, sloths hang upside down, resting for hours at a time. The bright colors of the tiny poison dart frog warn other animals that it is poisonous and should not be eaten. There are also many brightly colored birds such as toucans, parrots, and macaws. Other common animals throughout rainforests include ants, beetles, snakes, and bats.

The shoebill is a huge species of bird found in the rainforest of the Congo.

compare and contrast

How is the animal life in tropical rainforests like that in other forests? How is it different?

Poison dart frogs are native to the Amazon Rainforest.

The Amazon Rainforest

The world's largest rainforest is the Amazon Rainforest. Its plant and animal life is rich. Almost three-fourths of all the plant species in the world grow there.

Hummingbirds, toucans, and parrots are among the many colorful Amazonian birds. Reptiles include the anaconda (a huge snake that crushes its victims), the poisonous coral snake, and alligators. Giant butterflies are among the most spectacular of the insects.

The forest giant owl is a species of butterfly that lives from Mexico down to the Amazon River. Their wingspan can reach about 6.7 inches (17 cm) wide.

The capybara is the largest rodent in the world.

Mammals include nutria, great anteaters, and many monkey species. The capybara, a rodent that can weigh more than 110 pounds (50 kilograms), lives there. So does the tapir, a hoofed mammal that looks somewhat like a pig. A variety of fish, including the pirarucu—which weighs up to 325 pounds (150 kg)—and the giant catfish, swim in the Amazon River. Silver carp, neon tetras, and piranhas are shipped to tropical fish stores throughout the world. The electric eel is a dangerous fish capable of discharging up to 500 volts.

Consider This

Why do you think the Amazon Rainforest has so much diversity?

People of the Rainforest

People have lived in rainforests for thousands of years. These include the Yanomami and the Kayapó of the Amazon Rainforest, the Bambuti of the Ituri Forest of central Africa, the Kombai in Indonesia, and the Penan in Malaysia.

The Kombai of Indonesia survive by hunting and gathering. They still make bows and arrows for hunting.

There are about 32,000 Yanomami people. They live in a very small section of the Amazon Rainforest.

Many rainforest peoples were forced to move or to change their way of life as they came into contact with people from the outside world. However, there are still some groups that have maintained their traditional culture. There are still others that are considered "uncontacted," or undiscovered. These are people who are located so remotely that they have yet to be encountered or who have intentionally been left alone by outsiders.

Human rights organizations have called on governments and the companies that operate in the rainforests to protect the rights of the native peoples in these areas. Conflicts continue even though some countries have set aside protected areas for the tribes to live in.

Consider This

What rights for rainforest peoples might need protecting?

Life in a Tropical Rainforest

Millions of people live in the forests. For them the forests are sources of food, shelter, and other materials. A tropical rainforest is a delicate network of relationships between plants and animals. Many plants, for instance, rely on animals to spread their **pollen** from flower to flower. At the same time, animals may depend on plants for their food and shelter.

Some sloths have green fur. The color is caused by algae that live in the sloth's fur. Sloths get nutrients from the algae, and the green coloring helps them blend into their leafy surroundings.

Even people who live far away from tropical rainforests are affected by the forests. Many rainforest plants are used as medicines to help treat diseases. Quinine, which is used to fight malaria, comes from rainforest plants. So does paclitaxel, which is used to fight some cancers. Scientists believe there are many more plants there that will help treat or even cure serious diseases. In addition, products such as fruits, nuts, rubber, rattan, and wood come from rainforests.

WORD WISE

POLLEN IS THE SUBSTANCE THAT CAUSES PLANTS TO FORM SEEDS. NEW PLANTS THEN CAN GROW FROM THE SEEDS.

Tropical rainforests play a big role Earth's **water cycle**. They help to control the water supply of the areas where they grow. They do this by absorbing the constant rain and then releasing it slowly back into the atmosphere. Some of the water is released steadily into rivers. Many people rely on the rivers for their water supply and to irrigate their crops. Some of the water is released back into the air through evaporation. This keeps the air moist and leads to more rain.

Water is constantly on the move all over the world, but especially in a damp tropical rainforest.

Rainforests are among Earth's major sources of oxygen. Life would be very different without them.

Tropical rainforests are sometimes called the "lungs of the planet." Like all green plants, rainforest plants absorb carbon dioxide gas from the atmosphere and produce oxygen. They do this through the process of photosynthesis. Because the number of plants in the rainforests is so huge, the forests produce much of the world's oxygen, which animals and people need to live.

WORD WISE

THE WATER CYCLE IS THE CONTINUOUS MOVEMENT OF EARTH'S WATER THROUGH THE AIR, ON LAND, AND IN THE GROUND.

Are Tropical Forests in Danger?

There are many poor countries in and around tropical rainforests. Some poor countries sell the wood and other resources of rainforests to make much-needed money. This often means that entire sections of the forest are destroyed. Rainforests are also cut down to provide land for farming.

Slash-and-burn agriculture is common in rainforest areas. It consists of cutting trees and other vegetation, burning what is left, and then planting crops. Because of poor soil, many such areas can support only two or three agricultural plantings. After that the soil's nutrients are exhausted and the land is abandoned.

The loss of rainforests endangers many plants and animals that live nowhere else in the world. Over time, some of these plants and animals may become extinct, or die out completely.

Slash-and-burn farming has greatly reduced the amount of land the Amazon Rainforest covers.

compare and contrast

What does slash-and-burn agriculture have in common with the cutting down of rainforests? How might its effects be different?

The Amazon river dolphin is an endangered rainforest animal.

Clearing rainforest land also disrupts the water cycle. Rainwater washes away quickly instead of being stored in the plants and returned slowly to the atmosphere. Eventually, rain falls less often, and the region may experience drought.

The destruction of rainforests also affects the environment of the rest of the world. When forests are burned, massive amounts of carbon dioxide escape into the atmosphere. This carbon dioxide contributes to a problem known as global warming. Global warming is the gradual rise in Earth's average surface temperature. It happens because the extra greenhouse gases—such as carbon dioxide—that people have added to Earth's atmosphere trap in extra heat.

It's illegal to cut down large sections of the Amazon Rainforest for farming, but it still happens.

People need to protect Earth's tropical rainforests. They are important to the plants, animals, and people that call them home, but they also have a huge impact on people all over the world.

Cutting down rainforests also contributes to global warming in another way. Trees use carbon dioxide when they make their own food. Fewer trees mean that less carbon dioxide is being taken out of the atmosphere.

Consider This

Of the many things tropical rainforests do, which do you think is most important?

Glossary

absorb To take in or suck or swallow up.
atmosphere The layer of gas that surrounds Earth.
bacteria Tiny living things that can be found in all natural environments and consist of a single cell.
cancer A disease that causes certain cells in the body to grow out of control.
carbon dioxide A gas that animals breathe out and plants use in photosynthesis.
climate The weather found in a certain place over a long period of time.
debris The remains of something broken down or destroyed.
drought A shortage of rain over a long period of time.
extinct No longer existing.
fern A flowerless green plant with leaves that look like feathers.
fungi A group of simple living things that are neither plants nor animals. Mushrooms, molds, and yeasts are fungi.
irrigate To supply with water by artificial means.
malaria A serious disease spread by mosquitoes.
mammal A type of living thing with a backbone and fur or hair. Female mammals produce milk to feed their babies.
moss A small, seedless plant that often grows in moist, shady places.
oxygen A gas that animals need to breathe and plants produce during photosynthesis.
photosynthesis The process in which green plants use sunlight to make their own food.
rattan Stems from a climbing palm that are used to make furniture and baskets.
temperate Having a climate that is usually mild without extremely cold or extremely hot temperatures.
tract A large stretch of land.
vegetation Plant life or cover.

For More Information

Books

Johnson, Cheryl. *Creatures of the Rainforest*. Naperville, IL: Sourcebooks Explore, 2026.

Pincus, Meeg. *Poison Dart Frogs in the Wild*. Ann Arbor, MI: Cherry Lake Publishing, 2026.

Websites

Layers of the Rainforest
www.sciencefacts.net/layers-of-the-rainforest.html
This detailed website offers more information about the layers of the rainforest.

Rainforest Habitat
kids.nationalgeographic.com/nature/habitats/article/rain-forest
Learn more about Earth's rainforests with National Geographic Kids.

Index